THE FIRST EASTER

Rachel Billington
Illustrated by Elisa Trimby

William B. Eerdmans Publishing Company
Grand Rapids, Michigan

Text copyright © 1987 by Rachel Billington
Illustrations copyright © 1987 by Elisa Trimby
First published 1987 in Great Britain by Constable & Co Ltd
This edition published 1987 through special arrangement with Constable
by William B. Eerdmans Publishing Company
255 Jefferson Avenue SE, Grand Rapids, Michigan 49503
All rights reserved
Printed in Great Britain
ISBN 0-8028-3637-2

THE SUN rose hot above the golden city of Jerusalem. The stone buildings with their flat roofs clung close to the mountain top. From far away, the city seemed part of the sandy mountainous range, the distant desert. Only a few dark trees marked gardens around its walls.

A young man paused in his journey towards it. He came from the North, from Nazareth and Galilee where the grass grew green round lakes as big as seas and in the spring the hillsides were covered with flowers.

When this young man stopped, hundreds of other people stopped too because this was Jesus, about to make his entrance into Jerusalem. For three years he had been travelling round the countryside teaching people how to obey God's commandments. The Romans, who ruled most of this part of the world, did not like any young man who drew great numbers of followers round him. They feared he might lead a Jewish rebellion and would have liked to kill him.

But they could do nothing while Jesus was followed by admiring crowds. There were men, including his special followers, the disciples. There were women, including Mary, his mother, and there were children, running everywhere, excited and noisy. It was not just that he performed miracles, turning water into wine and making vast amounts of food where there'd only been a few loaves of bread. Recently, he had actually brought to life a dead man whose name was Lazarus.

Jesus was a hero and his followers were eager to spread his fame to Jerusalem. But one of the most important lessons he taught was that we should be humble, so he would not enter the city like a powerful king. Instead he ordered two of his disciples to bring him a young donkey. He mounted the donkey and continued the journey on its back; this might have looked ridiculous if it had been anyone else, for his feet nearly touched the ground. But Jesus didn't care about things like that. Nor did the crowds.

AS HE approached the city walls, hundreds of people poured out to greet him, shouting, "Hosanna to the Son of David!" and "Blessed is he that comes in the name of the Lord!" They spread palm leaves in his path and tore off their cloaks to lay in front of him. Some asked, "Who is he?" and others answered, "This is Jesus, the prophet from Nazareth."

All day Jesus was surrounded by crowds. He told them that he would die, although no-one quite understood what he meant. He said, "I am the light that has come into the world and anyone who believes in me will not live in darkness." When evening came, he left the city and went back to the village of Bethany with his twelve disciples.

EARLY NEXT morning, Jesus set off for Jerusalem again. On his way he passed a fig tree and since he'd had no breakfast, he searched for some fruit. But there was none, which made him angry because it was pretending to be something it was not. So he swore that the tree should never bear fruit again.

When they reached the city Jesus went straight to the temple and was made even more angry. For it was being used as a market place with people buying and selling oxen and sheep and doves and exchanging money. So he beat the shop-keepers and flung the money to the floor and overturned the tables. He cried out, "Take away these things! You mustn't use my Father's house as if it were a shop! You have turned a place of prayer into a den of thieves!"

Soon people heard Jesus was in the temple and the blind and the lame came to him to be healed. Each time he cured somebody, the children shouted, "Hosanna to the son of David!" This annoyed the priests and scribes and they said to Jesus, "Just listen to what these foolish children are saying!" But Jesus answered calmly, "Have you never read, 'The truth comes out of the mouths of children and babies'?" And he continued teaching in the temple, even though he knew the priests were plotting to kill him.

Once more when night fell he walked the two miles out to Bethany.

The next morning he came back to the temple and spent all day teaching the people that they should trust in God, who was his father.

The Pharisees, who were the cleverest men in the city, thought they would trick him into saying something against the government. Then he could be arrested. Pretending to be

friendly, they asked him, "Master, we know you
tell us to follow God's way of life, to pay him tribute.
Then should we pay tribute to Caesar who is our ruler?"

But Jesus saw their wicked plan and said, "Why do you
try and trap me, you hypocrites? Show me a coin." They
showed him a penny and he said, "Whose face is on it?"

They answered, "Caesar's."

Then Jesus said, "Give to Caesar the things that are
Caesar's and to God the things that are God's." So the
Pharisees gave up for the time being and allowed Jesus to
continue preaching.

THE FOLLOWING day Jesus remained in Bethany. He
was seated at table when Mary, the sister of Lazarus
whom he'd raised from the dead, brought out an alabaster jar
which was filled with expensive scented oil. She poured the
oil over him and rubbed his feet and dried them with her hair.

The disciples were shocked at the waste and protested,
"You could have sold the oil for a great deal of money and
given it to the poor." But Jesus defended her: "Leave the
woman alone. She's behaved quite properly. You will always
have the poor to look after but I'll be soon gone from you.
Her anointing will prepare my body for burial. Indeed she
will always be remembered for her kindness."

That very night one of the disciples, called Judas Iscariot,
went to the chief priests and captains of the guard and said,
"What will you pay me if I betray Jesus?" And they said,
"Thirty pieces of silver."

Judas accepted their offer and promised to let them know
when Jesus was not protected by the crowd.

DESPITE THE danger, Jesus was determined to celebrate the Jewish feast of Passover inside Jerusalem. He told the disciples to go ahead of him and they would find a man holding a jug of water who would lead them to a large upstairs room. There they must prepare everything for the meal.

In the evening Jesus joined them for what we call now "the last supper". But first he filled a basin with water and washed and dried the feet of the apostles. When Simon Peter tried to stop him, he explained that they must be washed by him to be made pure inside, but that there was one of them who he could not make clean. By this he meant Judas, because Jesus knew Judas was going to betray him.

After this he took up some bread. He blessed it, broke it and gave it to the disciples saying, "Take this and eat it in my memory." Then he held up a cup of wine and said, "This is my blood which will be shed so that your sins may be forgiven. Drink it in memory of me." They talked far into the night and Jesus prepared them for when he would be gone. He said, "You must love one another as I have loved you."

Then Peter asked, "Where are you going?"

Jesus answered, "I'm going somewhere you can't follow."

"I'll follow you anwhere," Peter insisted, "to prison or to
death. I would die for you!" But Jesus shook his head. "I tell
you, before tonight is over and the cock has crowed twice,
you will deny that you know me three times."

Peter refused to believe it but Jesus told them how they
would all run away, leaving him alone — except that because
he was with God, his father, he was never really alone. He
told them, "You will have many sufferings in this world but
take heart, I will be with you."

It was the middle of the night as they finished supper
and, before they left the safety of that upstairs room, they
sang a hymn.

THEN JESUS went to a garden which he always visited when he wanted to be quiet or to pray. It was called Gethsemane, at the foot of the Mount of Olives. He told his disciples to wait for him and went further under the trees with Peter and James and John.

He grew more and more sorrowful, because the time had nearly come when he must die. For God had sent him to earth so that by his life he could show us how to live, and by his death he could redeem our sins. So he went alone

deeper into the darkness, but he asked his disciples to keep him company by staying awake. He crouched down on the ground and prayed to God. "Father," he said, "You can do anything. If it is possible, take this cup of suffering from me. But not because I ask, but because it is what you want."

Out of the night sky, an angel appeared, bringing him light and strength. Even so, he was in such agony that, as he prayed, he began to sweat and the drops fell darkly to the ground like drops of blood. So he went back to the disciples, but he found them sleeping, for they were tired and unhappy.

"Oh Peter!" Jesus cried reproachfully, "Couldn't you watch with me for one hour?"

Three times Jesus went to pray and three times he came back to find the disciples asleep. The third time he said, "Get up now. I am betrayed into the hands of sinners. Look, and you'll see them coming!"

JUDAS WAS approaching through the olive trees with the High Priest and a great band of priests and pharisees and soldiers. They carried lanterns and sticks and swords.

Judas said to the soldiers, "The man you want is the man I shall kiss." And he went up to Jesus and kissed him, saying, "Master, master."

Jesus looked at him calmly, "Friend, why are you here? To betray the son of man with a kiss?" Then he turned to the priests, "Who are you looking for?"

They answered, "Jesus of Nazareth."

Jesus said, "I am he. Arrest me but leave my followers alone."

When Peter saw what was happening, he drew his sword and cut off the right ear of the High Priest's servant. But Jesus told him, "Put your sword back into its sheath. He who lives by the sword will die by the sword." And he touched the servant's ear so that it was healed again. "Don't you realise, if I prayed to God, my Father, twelve legions of angels would come to rescue me?"

Then he turned to his captors. "Why have you brought swords and sticks as if I were a thief? You have seen me teaching in the temple every day but you did not touch me. Now it is night and you have the power of darkness and evil." As the soldiers prepared to lead him off, the disciples ran away, frightened. So Jesus was taken all by himself to the palace of Caiaphas, the High Priest.

Later on, Peter and one other disciple found enough courage to follow and wait in a courtyard where a fire had been lit. After a while one of the maidservants recognised Peter. She said, "This man was also with Jesus of Nazareth. Aren't you a disciple?" Peter denied it saying, "Woman, I am not.

I do not know him. I don't know what you're talking about!"
And he hurried away just as the cock crowed once.

Soon after, another maid recognised him, saying to the
people around, "This fellow was with Jesus of Nazareth."
And again Peter denied it, even more fiercely.

About an hour later a manservant passed by. "Here is one
of Jesus' followers," he said confidently. "You can tell he
comes from Galilee by his accent. I saw you in the garden,
didn't I?" Peter denied it angrily, 'I don't know what you're
talking about!" As he spoke the cock crowed a second time
and he remembered the last supper when Jesus had told him
that before the cock crowed twice he would deny him three
times. He rushed outside and wept bitterly.

MEANWHILE, inside the palace, Jesus was being questioned by Caiaphas and the chief priests. They wanted to send him to the Roman governor of Jerusalem, Pontius Pilate, who had the power to execute him. They found witnesses who told all kinds of lies about what Jesus had said and done. Jesus himself would not say a word.

At length they said to him, "Tell us, are you the Messiah, the Son of God?" And Jesus answered, "You have said it. Nevertheless I tell you that you will see the son of man sitting at the right hand of God, trailing clouds of glory."

At this the priests tore their clothes and screamed out. "Now he has blasphemed. We don't need witnesses anymore.

He deserves to die!" They spat in Jesus' face and beat him and blindfolded him, saying mockingly, "Since you're a prophet, tell us who it was who just hit you?" In this way he was led off to Pontius Pilate.

Pilate questioned him in the hall of judgement and asked him, "Are you king of the Jews?" Jesus answered, "My kingdom is not in this world." And he said more which made Pilate realise he was innocent.

Just at that moment Pilate received a message from his wife saying she had had a terrible nightmare about the good man he was holding prisoner and that he must release him.

It was the custom at Passover to release one prisoner. A crowd had gathered now that it was morning and when he asked who he should let go, they cried "Barabbas!" Barabbas was a common thief, certainly guilty. When Pilate suggested, "Let me release Jesus of Nazareth." They screamed back, "Crucify him! Crucify him!"

Still Pilate hesitated and said, "I will punish him and then let him go, for he is not guilty. So Jesus was stripped and whipped and afterwards a scarlet robe was placed round his shoulders and a crown made of thorny branches on his head and the soldiers mocked him shouting, "Hail, King of the Jews!"

In this fashion, Pilate had him led before the crowd again, and again said that he was innocent and should be released. But the crowd cried even more furiously, "Crucify him! Crucify him!" Pilate replied, "Shall I crucify your king?" But the crowd answered, "We have no king but Caesar!"

So then Pilate ordered a bowl of water to be brought and he washed his hands in it, saying, "Look, I am innocent of the blood of this good man. And the crowd cried, "His blood will be on us and on our children!"

JESUS WAS given his cross to carry and set off up the hill where he was to be crucified. The soldiers came with him and the crowd behind them which made it a long procession winding its way through the narrow streets of Jerusalem. The road was uphill, the cross was made of heavy wood and Jesus was weak from his beating. So a young man called Simon was told to help him carry it.

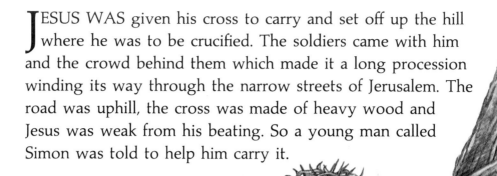

At length they arrived at the hill called Calvary and in Hebrew, Golgotha, meaning the place of the skull. There Jesus' cross was set up between the crosses of two common thieves. The soldiers offered him drugged wine to drink and he was nailed to the cross. But he said, "Father, forgive them for they know not what they do."

Then the soldiers rolled dice to see who would get Jesus' long cloak.

Meanwhile Pilate had a sign nailed above Jesus' head which read, "Jesus, King of the Jews." This made the chief priests very angry. They cried out, "It should read 'This is Jesus who said he was the King of the Jews.'"

Then one of the thieves who was also being crucified shouted out, "If you really are the son of God, why don't you save yourself and us too?" Before Jesus could answer, the other thief spoke up, "Aren't you afraid of God, seeing as you're on the way to death? Besides, we deserved our sentences, unlike this man who's done nothing wrong." Then he turned his head to Jesus, "Will you remember me when you enter your kingdom?"

To which Jesus answered, "Truly, I say to you, this day you will be with me in Paradise."

At the foot of the cross, there stood three women, all called Mary. Mary, the mother of Jesus, Mary Magdalen and another Mary. They were crying miserably so that Jesus, despite his own suffering, took pity on them. He called for the disciple, John, who he loved most and made him stand by his mother, Mary.

He said, "Woman, behold your son. Son, behold your mother." Then he knew John would care for her when he was dead.

AT MIDDAY, a strange darkness came over the sky blotting out the sun.

At three o'clock, Jesus called out with a loud voice, "My God, My God, why have you forsaken me!" And some thought he was crying out for help. Then he said, "I am thirsty" and a soldier poked up to him a stick with a sponge dipped in sour vinegar on the end. He drank and immediately afterwards said, "It is finished." But just before he died, he suddenly lifted up his head and shouted for all to hear, "Father, into your hands, I commend my spirit."

Now it really was the end. Jesus had died. His head fell onto his chest. And the earth itself reacted. Earthquakes made the ground rock and split apart. The curtain in front of the holiest part of the temple where Jesus had taught was torn in two and tombs cracked open.

When the soldiers saw all this, they were afraid and said to each other, "Surely this was the Son of God."

ONCE PILATE was certain of Jesus' death he gave permission for a certain Joseph of Arimathea, who was a secret follower of Jesus, to take down the body from the cross. The Jews wanted to do it that very night because the next day was the Sabbath when they must only rest. So they took out the nails from his hands and feet and carried him to a new tomb prepared for him in a garden. There they were met by Mary, his mother and other women. They wished to anoint him with spices and herbs but could not do it till the day after the Sabbath. So they left him alone.

But the chief priests and pharisees were worried because Jesus had said, "In three days I will rise again." So they went to Pilate and asked him to put a guard on the tomb in case Jesus' disciples stole his body away. Pilate agreed and a huge boulder was rolled against the sepulchre, which was cut out of rock like a cave, and a soldier was set to guard it.

Jesus' body lay in that dark place, wound in the white sheets of death, for that night and the following day and night.

EARLY ON Sunday morning, so early that the sun had not yet risen and the air was still misty, Mary Magdalen went with two other women to the sepulchre. They carried spices with which to anoint the body of Jesus. As they went, staying close together, for the world looked strange in this hour before dawn, they wondered how they would roll back the stone that covered the mouth of the tomb.

Imagine their surprise when they saw the stone gone and the tomb gaping open! Nervously, they went, step by step, into the dank darkness.

Suddenly they were surrounded with light and an angel clothed in a long white robe, appeared. Terrified, they bowed their heads to the ground. But the angel spoke to them gently:

"Do not be afraid. I know that you are looking for Jesus of Nazareth who was crucified. But why are you looking for the living among the dead? He is not here. He is risen as he said he would. Come, behold the place where they laid him."

The women looked and saw the empty tomb and sheets in which he had been wrapped.

The angel continued, "Remember what he told you when he was still in Galilee: "The son of man must be given into the hands of sinful men and be crucified and on the third day rise again." And the women remembered his words.

The angel commanded them, "Go quickly now and tell the disciples and Peter that Jesus has risen from the dead."

With that the angel disappeared, taking the brightness with him. But now Mary Magdalen and the other two were filled with excitement. They rushed out of the sepulchre and out of the garden and, although it was after dawn now and there were people about, they did not tell anyone the news until they found the disciples.

Peter and John immediately ran to the sepulchre with Mary Magdalen following more slowly behind. Hardly knowing what to believe, the two disciples walked into the quiet darkness and saw for themselves the empty tomb and the cloths left abandoned on the ground.

After they had left in amazement, Mary Magdalen stayed behind, weeping. Suddenly she sensed someone behind her. She turned round and saw a man standing at the mouth of the cave. He said "Woman, why are you weeping? Who are you looking for?"

Thinking he was the gardener, she sobbed, "You have carried my lord away. Tell me where you have laid him and I will come and fetch him."

The man said, "Mary." And all at once, Mary Magdalen realised it was Jesus himself and she cried out joyfully, "Master!"

THAT SAME day two of the disciples were walking to a
village called Emmaus which was about seven miles from
Jerusalem. They were discussing the extraordinary events of
the day when a stranger joined them. At least they thought
it was a stranger.

He said to them, "What are you talking about and why
do you look so sad?"

They answered, "You must indeed be a stranger to Jerusalem not to know the things that have been happening."

Jesus asked, "What things?" So they told him the story of Jesus of Nazareth and how he had been crucified and buried. And how that very day an angel had told some women that he was alive.

Seeing they were not certain whether to believe it, Jesus stayed with them and talked to them. Eventually they arrived at Emmaus and Jesus was about to continue but the disciples invited him to stop and eat supper with them.

As they ate together, Jesus broke bread and gave it to them. And their eyes were opened and they knew who he was. But as they recognised him, he vanished. So they hurried back to Jerusalem and described what had happened.

That same evening, the disciples were gathered together to eat their supper. The door of the room was locked for fear they would be arrested.

Suddenly Jesus stood among them. He said, "Peace be with you!" And he scolded them for their lack of belief. But they were terrified and thought he was a ghost.

So then he told them to touch him, "For a ghost doesn't have flesh and blood as I do." And he showed them his hands and his feet where the nails had been and his side where the sword had pierced.

But still the disciples hardly dared to believe in such a miracle. So he took some grilled fish and ate them for certainly ghosts can't eat. At length he left saying, "Let the Holy Spirit come upon you. If you forgive sins they shall be forgiven."

One of the disciples, called Thomas, was not there when Jesus came.

He said, "Until I can touch the marks of the nails in his hands and the wound in his side, I will not believe he's alive."

Eight days later, the disciples were gathered together once more behind locked doors, when Jesus appeared in the middle of the room. "Peace be with you," he said first. And then turned to "doubting" Thomas, "Reach out and put your fingers in my palms and your hand in my side."

Thomas was filled with faith. He cried, "My Lord and my God!" And Jesus was pleased. Yet he said, "Thomas, you have believed because you have seen me. But happy are those who have not seen and still believe!"

Then Jesus told them not to be afraid but to go out to Galilee where he would reappear. And he himself took them as far as Bethany before he blessed them and went away.

NOT LONG afterwards, Peter and Thomas and several other disciples were fishing on the Sea of Tiberias which is in Galilee. They spent all night in the boat and caught nothing. As dawn broke they saw a man standing on the shore. He called to them, "Have you caught anything, friends?"

"Nothing," they answered.

"Cast your net over the right side and you'll make a catch."

They did so and at once the net was so full of fish that they couldn't pull it out of the water.

Then John, who Jesus particularly loved, recognised the stranger. "It is the Lord!" he cried. And Peter jumped into the water to get to him more quickly, while the others followed in their boat.

When they reached the shore, they found a fire already made with bread and fish on it and Jesus told them to bring up their fish. So they dragged in the net, which didn't break even though they had caught one hundred and fifty three fish.

After they'd eaten, Jesus spoke to them, asking Peter three times whether he loved him until Peter became upset and said, "Lord, you who know everything, know that I love you." So Jesus told them how they must look after his people when he had gone.

He said, "You must go, all of you, out into the world and preach the gospel to everyone you meet. He who believes in me and is baptised will be saved and he who refuses to believe will be punished."

LATER THE eleven disciples went further into Galilee and climbed to the top of a mountain where Jesus had arranged to meet them. When he came they all worshipped him but some still doubted.

Yet again he spoke but this time it was with special strength because these were to be his last words. "I have been given power over heaven and earth. Therefore I tell you to go out and teach all nations, baptising the people in the name of the Father, Son and Holy Ghost. Teach them to love and serve God, which means they should behave as I have taught you. And remember, I am with you always, even until the end of the world!"

Then, stretching out his hands, he blessed them. And as he did so, he was carried up out of their sight into heaven, where he is seated at the right hand of God. At last the disciples were inspired with true faith and they made the long journey to Jerusalem filled with joy.

At first they prayed in the temple, praising and glorifying God. But as their courage increased, they went out and preached throughout the world. For the spirit of Jesus was with them wherever they went.

SO ENDS the story of the First Easter. Jesus entered Jerusalem, was cruelly put to death but rose again from the dead. Through his life and death his disciples learned how to lead their lives. And they, in their turn, have passed the message down to us.

AUTHOR'S NOTE

In retelling for children the complicated story of
Jesus' triumph, death and resurrection, which is
made more complicated by the different or even
contradictory accounts given by Matthew, Mark,
Luke and John, I have not relied on any one gospel
but followed whichever seemed to serve the
natural flow of the narrative.

Rachel Billington